Reading Placement Tests

Easy Assessments to Determine
Students' Levels in Phonics, Vocabulary,
and Reading Comprehension

1st Grade

SCHOLASTIC
PROFESSIONAL **B**OOKS

NEW YORK • TORONTO • LONDON • AUCKLAND • SYDNEY
MEXICO CITY • NEW DELHI • HONG KONG • BUENOS AIRES

Cover design by Josué Castilleja
Cover art by Royce Fitzgerald
Interior illustrations by Kate Flanagan
Interior design by LDL Designs

Pages 23–31 © CORE.

Table of Contents

Overview

The Diagnostic Placement Tests and Phonics Survey for Grade 1 are designed as entry-level assessments for your students. The Diagnostic Placement Test is intended to be used at the beginning of the school year and has three main purposes:

- to determine each child's level of proficiency in reading, based on grade-level skills.
- to identify specific instructional needs for individual students and for the group as a whole.
- to provide a baseline from which to measure a child's growth in reading.

During the first weeks of school, it is important to determine children's reading levels. The Diagnostic Placement Test, designed to be administered to groups of students, measures important skills in Phonics/Phonological Awareness, grade-level Vocabulary, and Reading Comprehension. For most students, results from this test will provide the initial screening information you'll need for instructional planning. After completing the Diagnostic Placement Test, you may want to collect more information about some children by administering the CORE Phonics Survey* (pages 23–31) to individuals. This survey measures alphabet skills, reading and decoding skills, and spelling skills. Assessment information from prior years may also provide valuable information about each child's current level of proficiency and his or her instructional needs for the coming year.

> **Phonological awareness** is an umbrella term that includes phonemic awareness, or awareness of words at the phoneme level. It also includes an awareness of word units larger than the phoneme.
>
> Phonological awareness includes the following (Eldridge, 1995):
>
> - words within sentences
> - rhyming units within words
> - beginning and ending sounds within words
> - syllables within words
> - phonemes, or sounds, within words (phonemic awareness)
> - features of individual phonemes such as how the mouth, tongue, vocal cords, and teeth are used to produce the sound

Description of the Placement Tests

Directions for administering and scoring the tests appear on the next few pages. The Diagnostic Placement Test has three sections:

Phonics/Phonological Awareness This first part of the test assesses skills in phonics and phonological awareness. (10 Questions)

* © 1999 by CORE.

Vocabulary This part of the test assesses children's familiarity with grade-level vocabulary words. All vocabulary words are tested in sentence context. (10 Questions)

Comprehension This last part of the test assesses children's comprehension of reading selections, both fiction and nonfiction. Children respond to comprehension questions based on fundamental grade-level skills. (5 Questions)

All questions on the Diagnostic Placement Test are in multiple-choice format. Each test item has three answer choices. In the following pages, you will find directions for administering the tests. Then turn to pages 19–22 for directions for scoring the tests and using the results.

Directions for Administering the Tests

The Diagnostic Placement Test is designed to be administered to a group, in either one or multiple sittings. These tests are not intended to be timed; allow as much time as children need to complete each part of the test. However, for planning purposes, the chart below shows the estimated time required for administering the test.

Estimated Time for Administering Tests

Phonics	Vocabulary	Comprehension	Total
10 minutes	10 minutes	10 minutes	30 minutes

When you are ready to begin, make sure each child has a stapled copy of the reproducible test and two pencils. (The Student Test Pages consist of a cover page and seven test pages. They can be found on pages 11–18 in this book.) Before starting, have each child write his or her name on the cover.

On pages 6–10 in this book you will find step-by-step directions for administering the test. Directions printed in bold type are intended to be read aloud by you the teacher; all other directions are for the teacher only. Read the directions and questions aloud, as indicated, and give children time to respond to each question by circling one of three answer choices. (If children are not familiar with circling answers, you may want to demonstrate on the chalkboard.) Throughout the test, check frequently to make sure children are on the right page and are following directions correctly.

Step-by-Step
Test Administration Guide

PHONICS/PHONOLOGICAL AWARENESS

PART I: BEGINNING SOUNDS

Have children turn to page 2. Make sure they are on the right page.

Point to the star in the box at the top of the page. **Look at the pictures in the box: *pen, net, tie*. Which has the same beginning sound as *ten... ten*? Circle the one with the same beginning sound as *ten*.** (Pause for children to mark their answers.) **Which one has the same beginning sound as *ten*?** (Have a child provide the answer.) **That's correct. *Tie* begins with the same sound as *ten*. You should have circled the picture of the tie. Does anyone have any questions?** (Answer any questions that children might have. Then proceed with questions 1–4. Pause after each question for children to mark their answers.)

We are going to do a few more questions like this. Listen carefully.
1. **Move down to the next box. Look at the pictures: *rose, map, four*. Which has the same beginning sound as *more... more*? Circle your answer.**
2. **Move down to the next box. Look at the pictures: *pail, kite, bike*. Which has the same beginning sound as *pick... pick*? Circle your answer.**
3. **Move down to the next box. Look at the pictures: *nest, can, five*. Which has the same beginning sound as *fun... fun*? Circle your answer.**
4. **Move down to the next box. Look at the pictures: *mouse, zipper, comb*. Which has the same beginning sound as *zoom... zoom*? Circle your answer.**

PART II: ENDING SOUNDS

Have children turn to page 3. Make sure they are on the right page.

Point to the star in the box at the top of the page. **Look at the pictures in the box: *dog, sock, bed*. Which has the same ending sound as *seed... seed*? Circle the one with the same ending** sound as *seed.* (Pause for children to mark their answers.) **Which one has the same ending sound as *seed*?** (Have a child provide the answer.) **That's correct. *Bed* ends with the same sound as *seed*. You should have circled the picture of the bed. Does anyone have any questions?** (Answer any questions that children might have. Then proceed with questions 5–7. Pause after each question for children to mark their answers.)

We are going to do a few more questions like this. Listen carefully.

5. **Move down to the next box. Look at the pictures: *ham, goat, top.* Which has the same ending sound as *meet...meet*? Circle your answer.**

6. **Move down to the next box. Look at the pictures: *truck, key, bowl.* Which has the same ending sound as *book... book*? Circle your answer.**

7. **Move down to the next box. Look at the pictures: *penny, bridge, jar.* Which has the same ending sound as *page... page*? Circle your answer.**

PART III: VOWELS

Have children turn to page 4. Make sure they are on the right page.

Point to the star in the box at the top of the page, where you see the picture of a pot. Look at the words: *net, not, Nat.* Which word rhymes with *pot... pot*? Circle the word that rhymes with *pot*. (Pause for children to mark their answers.) **Which word rhymes with *pot*?** (Have a child provide the answer.) **That's correct. The word *not* rhymes with *pot*. You should have circled the middle word, *not*. Does anyone have any questions?** (Answer any questions that children might have. Then proceed with questions 8–10. Pause after each question for children to mark their answers.)

We are going to do a few more questions like this. Listen carefully.

8. **Move down to the next box, where you see the picture of a man. Look at the words: *pan, pen, pin.* Which word rhymes with *man... man*? Circle your answer.**

9. **Move down to the next box, where you see the picture of a hut. Look at the words: *bit, boat, but.* Which word rhymes with *hut... hut*? Circle your answer.**

10. **Move down to the next box, where you see the picture of soap. Look at the words: *rap, ripe, rope.* Which word rhymes with *soap . . . soap*? Circle your answer.**

VOCABULARY

PART I: SIGHT WORDS

Have children turn to page 5. Make sure they are on the right page.

Point to the star in the box at the top of the page. There are three words in the box. I am going to read a word. Then I will use the word in a sentence. You are to find the word I say and draw a circle around the word. Let's try the first one. The word is *dog*. *I like my dog*. Circle the word *dog*. (Pause for children to mark their answers.) **Which word is *dog*?** (Have a child provide the answer. Then hold up the book and point to the correct answer so children can see it.) **That's correct. You should have circled the word in the middle. That word is *dog*, *d-o-g*. Does anyone have any questions?** (Answer any questions that children might have. Then proceed with questions 1–5. Pause after each question to give children time to mark their answers.)

We are going to do a few more questions like this. Listen carefully.
1. **Move down to the next box, where you see the picture of the sun. The word is *from*. I walked home from school. Circle the word *from*.**
2. **Move down to the next box, where you see the picture of the bell. The word is *what*. What is your name? Circle the word *what*.**
3. **Move down to the next box, where you see the picture of the shoe. The word is *jump*. Tim can jump high. Circle the word *jump*.**
4. **Move down to the next box, where you see the picture of the moon. The word is *today*. I had a good breakfast today. Circle the word *today*.**
5. **Move down to the next box, where you see the picture of the cup. The word is *should*. You should drink your milk. Circle the word *should*.**

PART II: WORD READING

Have children turn to page 6. Make sure they are on the right page.

Point to the star in the box at the top of the page. Look at the picture in the box. Then look at the words beside the picture. Which word names the picture? Circle the word that tells the name of the picture. (Pause for children to mark their answers.) **Which word names the pic-**

ture? (Have a child provide the answer. Then hold up the book and point to the correct answer so children can see it.) **That's correct. You should have circled the word *cat*. The picture shows a cat. Does anyone have any questions?** (Answer any questions that children might have.) **Now you will do the rest of the questions on this page in the same way. Look at the picture in each box. Circle the word that names the picture. You may begin.**

Allow a few minutes for children to complete items 6–10.

COMPREHENSION

Have children turn to page 7. Make sure they are on the right page.
In this part of the test, I am going to read some stories. After each story, I am going to ask you some questions. Listen carefully. The first story is about a cow named Clara. Let's begin.

Clara the Cow

Clara the Cow lives in a barn with lots of other cows. Clara likes her home and her friends, but she also likes to see new places. More than anything else, she loves flowers.

One day, Clara wandered away from the barn and took a walk down the road. Before long, she found a field of pretty flowers. "I like this place," she said. "I think I'll spend the day here." Clara smelled the flowers, listened to the birds singing, and ate some nice green grass. Then she started feeling drowsy, so she lay down to take a short nap.

When Clara woke up, it was almost dark. "Oh, my! I have to find the others," she thought. Clara walked and walked, but she couldn't find the other cows. She couldn't find the barn either. She was lost. Clara began to cry.

Just then Clara heard a bark. It was Bonnie, the dog from the farm.

"We missed you," said Bonnie. "Follow me to the barn."

Clara had never been so glad to see Bonnie.

Read questions 1 and 2. Pause after each to give children time to mark their answers.
Now I am going to ask you two questions about this story. Listen carefully.

1. Point to the box at the top of the page, where you see the small sun. Look at the pictures. Which picture shows what Clara likes best? Circle the picture that shows what Clara likes best.

2. Move down to the next box, where you see the bell. Look at the pictures. Who helped Clara find her way back to the barn? Circle the picture of the one who helped Clara.

When children are ready, have them turn to page 8. Make sure they are on the right page. Now I am going to read you another story. This story is about two friends named Maria and Cameron. Listen carefully.

Good Friends

Maria and Cameron are good friends, but they live in very different places.

    Maria lives in a big city. Her home is an apartment. She rides the bus to school every day. The city zoo is near her apartment. On Saturdays Maria likes to go to the zoo and visit the animals. If she needs to buy anything, Maria walks across the street to the store.

    Cameron lives on a farm in the country. His home is a farmhouse. He gets a ride to school every day in his father's truck. He does not live near a zoo, but he sees animals every day on his farm. Cameron likes to feed the chickens every morning. If he needs to buy anything, Cameron has to travel a long way to the nearest store.

Read questions 3 to 5. Pause after each to give children time to mark their answers.

Now I am going to ask you three questions about this story. Listen carefully.

3. Point to the box at the top of the page, where you see the small shoe. Look at the pictures. Which picture shows where Maria lives? Circle the picture that shows where Maria lives.

4. Move down to the next box, where you see the small moon. Look at the pictures. What is near Maria's home? Circle the picture of something that is near Maria's home.

5. Move down to the next box, where you see the cup. Look at the pictures. Which one shows how Cameron gets to school? Circle the picture that shows how Cameron gets to school.

You have now finished administering the Diagnostic Placement Test. Directions for scoring and evaluating the tests appear on pages 19–22. To gain more information on individual students' reading skills, you can administer the CORE Phonics Survey (pages 23–31).

Name _____   Date _____

Diagnostic Placement Test
Grade 1

Phonics

© 2002 by Scholastic Inc.

Phonics

Phonics

★	net not Nat
8.	pan pen pin
9.	bit boat but
10.	rap ripe rope

Vocabulary

★	go	dog	and
1.	for	time	from
2.	what	we	pet
3.	jump	name	stop
4.	may	today	they
5.	show	could	should

Vocabulary

★	cat cap let
6.	pig log pin
7.	bee are bear
8.	does fish ask
9.	window yellow woman
10.	funny money maybe

Comprehension

1.	
2.	

Comprehension

3.			
4.			
5.			

Scoring the Tests

To score the Diagnostic Placement Test, refer to the Answer Key below. Each test item should be scored correct or incorrect. You may mark each item on the test page, or you may use a Scoring Chart (see page 20). To find the total score for each part of the test or the total test, add the number of items answered correctly.

To use the Scoring Chart, make a copy of the chart for each child. Mark each correct answer by circling the item number on the chart. Mark each incorrect answer by drawing an X through the item number. To find the total score for each part of the test or the total test, add the number of items answered correctly.

To find the percentage score for each part of the test or total test, refer to the table at the back of this book (page 32). Find the number of correct answers in the left-hand column. Follow the row across to the appropriate column for the total number of items. For example, a child who answers 7 out of 10 items correctly in Phonics has achieved a Phonics score of 70 percent correct.

Mark the scores for each part of the test and the total test on the child's test book or on the scoring chart. Use the Placement Test Summary Chart (page 21) to record the results for all children in the class.

Answer Key

Phonics/Phonological Awareness
1. map (Initial Consonant Sounds)
2. pail (Initial Consonant Sounds)
3. five (Initial Consonant Sounds)
4. zipper (Initial Consonant Sounds)
5. goat (Final Consonant Sounds)
6. truck (Final Consonant Sounds)
7. bridge (Final Consonant Sounds)
8. pan (Short Vowels)
9. but (Short Vowels)
10. rope (Long Vowels)

Vocabulary
1. from
2. what
3. jump
4. today
5. should
6. pig
7. bear
8. fish
9. window
10. money

Comprehension
1. flowers (Character)
2. dog (Plot)
3. apartment building (Make Inferences)
4. zoo (Setting)
5. boy in pickup truck (Details)

Diagnostic Placement Test
Scoring Chart

Child's Name _____ Date _____

Test Section Test Item Numbers	Number of Correct Responses	Percentage Score
Phonics/Phonological Awareness 1 3 5 7 9 2 4 6 8 10	10	
Vocabulary 1 3 5 7 9 2 4 6 8 10	10	
Comprehension 1 2 3 4 5	5	
Total Test	25	
Comments/Notes		

Placement Test Summary Chart

Teacher Name _____   Grade _____

NAME	PHONICS	VOCABULARY	COMPREHENSION	TOTAL

Using the Results

Use the test scores from the Diagnostic Placement Test to determine each child's current level of reading proficiency and to help determine instructional plans for the beginning of the year. Information from other assessments may be used to support or supplement instructional decisions. For example, children may have different developmental needs in reading and writing.

To use the results of the Diagnostic Placement Test, evaluate each child's scores on the test. The total test scores may be used to identify those children who are reading below grade level, at grade level, or above grade level, as defined below.

A total test score of…	Suggests that…
Less than 60%	The child is reading below grade level.
60%–89%	The child is reading at grade level.
90% or higher	The child is reading above grade level.

Scores on each part of the test may be used to help determine instructional plans. For any part in which a child scores 60 percent or less, the child will probably need additional focused instruction. For example, a child might score 80 percent in Phonics, 50 percent in Vocabulary, and 70 percent in Comprehension. This child is probably at grade level in Phonics and Comprehension but will need additional help to improve Vocabulary.

To help pinpoint specific needs for children, you can refer to the Answer Key. For each test item in Phonics and Comprehension, the answer key lists the skill or strategy measured by the item. You may use this information to help identify a child's specific needs. For example, a child might answer four of ten Phonics items incorrectly, and all four items concern long and short vowels. This information might suggest that the child needs additional instruction in vowels and vowel sounds.

For any child whose test scores are ambiguous or seem inconclusive, additional, individualized assessment is recommended. You may want to administer the CORE Phonics Survey (page 23).

Follow-up

Many children develop reading skills rapidly and at different rates. The Diagnostic Placement Test provides an entry-level assessment and a baseline from which to judge children's progress. However, each child should be assessed periodically to monitor his or her progress and help make adjustments in instructional plans or grouping.

CORE Phonics Survey

WHAT The *CORE Phonics Survey* assesses the phonics and phonics-related skills that have a high rate of application in beginning reading. The survey presents a number of lists of letters and words for the student to identify or decode. Pseudowords, or made-up words, are included since the student must use decoding skills to pronounce these words correctly and cannot have memorized them. This assessment is best used to plan instruction for students in the primary grades and to develop instructional groups. It may be administered every four to six weeks.

WHY A student's ability to use knowledge of sound/letter correspondences (phonics) to decode words determines, in large measure, his or her ability to read individual words. A detailed assessment of a student's phonics skills points to areas in which the student is likely to benefit most from systematic, explicit phonics instruction. Also, knowing the skills that the student does possess will help in selecting reading tasks that offer the most effective reinforcement of those skills.

HOW Instructions for administering each part of the survey are included on the Record Form (pages 24–28). Students read from the Student Material (pages 29–31). To focus the student's attention on the part of the test being given, cover the other parts with a piece of paper. The Record Form shows the same material that appears on the Student Material, in a reduced size, so that you may easily record the student's responses.

Following administration, score each of the test parts and transfer the results to the first page of the Record Form under Skills Summary. Retest every four to six weeks but only on parts not yet mastered. Be aware of the student's behavior during testing. If the student is tiring or making many consecutive errors, discontinue testing at that time.

WHAT IT MEANS This test is a mastery test. It is expected that students will ultimately get all items correct.
• In five-item subtests, a student who misses *two or more items* would benefit from more direct instruction in the indicated element.
• In ten-item subtests, *three or more errors* warrant attention.

WHAT'S NEXT? Use the information to monitor phonics instruction and to design skill groups in direct instruction in the particular element measured.

CORE Phonics Survey Record Form

Name _____ Grade _____ Date _____

SKILL SUMMARY

Alphabet Skills

_____/26   Letter Names – uppercase

_____/26   Letter Names – lowercase

_____/23   Consonant sounds

_____/5   Long vowel sounds

_____/5   Short vowel sounds

Reading and Decoding Skills

_____/10   Short vowels in CVC words

_____/10   Short vowels, digraphs, and *-tch* trigraph

_____/20   Short vowels and consonant blends

_____/10   Long vowels

_____/10   Vowel diphthongs

_____/10   *r-* and *l-*controlled vowels

_____/24   Multisyllabic words

Spelling Skills

_____/5   Initial consonants

_____/5   Final consonants

_____/5   CVC words

_____/5   Long vowel words

Skills to review: _____

_____

Skills to teach: _____

_____

1. Letter Names—Uppercase

Say to the student: *Can you tell me the names of these letters?* If the student cannot name three or more consecutive letters, say: *Look at all of the letters and tell me which ones you do know.*

	D	A	N	S	X	Z	J	L	H
	T	Y	E	C	O	M	R	P	W
__/26	K	U	G	B	F	Q	V	I	

2. Letter Names—Lowercase

Say to the student: *Can you tell me the names of these letters?* If the student cannot name three or more consecutive letters, say: *Look at all of the letters and tell me which ones you do know.*

	d	a	n	s	x	z	j	l	h
	t	y	e	c	o	m	r	p	w
__/26	k	u	g	b	f	q	v	i	

3. Consonant Sounds

Say to the student: *Look at these letters. Can you tell me the sound each letter makes?* Be sure to ask if he or she knows of another sound for the letters *g* and *c*. If the sound given is correct, do not mark the Record Form. If it is incorrect, write the sound the student gives above each letter. If no sound is given, circle the letter. If the student cannot say the sound for three or more consecutive letters, say: *Look at all of the letters and tell me which sounds you do know.*

	d	l	n	s	x	z	j
	t	y	p	c	h	m	r
__/23	k	w	g	b	f	q	v

4. Vowel Sounds

Ask the student: *Can you tell me the sounds of each letter?* If the student names the letter, count it as the long vowel sound. Then ask: *Can you tell me the other sound for the letter?* The student should name the short vowel sound.

e __ __ i __ __ a __ __ o __ __ u __ __

l = long sound   s = short sound

Record "l" on the first line for the long sound (letter name) and "s" for the short sound on the second line. If the student makes an error, record the error over the letter.

_____/5   Long vowel sounds (count the number of *l*'s above)

_____/5   Short vowel sounds (count the number of *s*'s above)

5. Reading and Decoding

For items A through G, students must read both real and pseudowords (made-up words). For the first line of real words, tell the student: *I want you to read these words.* If the student cannot read two or more of the real words, do not administer the line of pseudowords. Go to the next set of items. Before asking the student to read the line of pseudowords, say: *Now I want you to read some made-up words. Do not try to make them sound like real words.*

A. Short vowels in CVC words

_____/5	sit	cat	get	but	hot	(real)
_____/5	vot	fut	dit	ket	lat	(pseudo)

B. Short vowels, digraphs, and *-tch* trigraph

_____/5	when	chop	thin	shut	match	(real)
_____/5	wheck	shom	thax	phitch	chud	(pseudo)

C. Short vowels and consonant blends

_____/5	stop	trap	quick	spell	plan	(real)
_____/5	stig	brab	qued	snop	dran	(pseudo)
_____/5	ring	fast	sank	limp	held	(real)
_____/5	mang	nast	wunk	kimp	jelt	(pseudo)

D. Long vowels

_____ /5	tape	Pete	cute	paid	feet	(real)
_____ /5	pofe	bine	joad	vay	soat	(pseudo)

E. Vowel diphthongs

_____ /5	few	down	toy	hawk	coin	(real)
_____ /5	moit	rew	fout	zoy	bawk	(pseudo)

F. *r*- and *l*-controlled vowels

_____ /5	bark	horn	chirp	roar	cold	(real)
_____ /5	ferm	murd	gair	dall	chail	(pseudo)

G. Multisyllabic words

Administer this item if the student is able to read most of the single-syllable real and pseudo-words in the previous items. Say to the student: *Now I want you to read down the first column of words. Each of the real words in this column has two syllables.* Point to the first column. If the student can read at least three out of eight of the words in this column, say: *Now I want you to read some made-up words. Do not try to make them sound like real words.* Point to the second column. Repeat the same procedure for the third column.

NOTE: The following made-up words can be pronounced in two ways: *sunop* (su-nop or sun-op); *wopam* (wo-pam or wop-am); *potife* (po-tife or pot-ife); *zuride* (zu-ride or zur-ide); and *zubo* (zu-bo or zub-o).

_____ /3	Closed-closed	kidnap	pugnad	quibrap
_____ /3	Closed silent *e*	compete	slifnate	prubkine
_____ /3	Open-closed	depend	sunop	wopam
_____ /3	Open-open	zero	zubo	yodu
_____ /3	Open silent *e*	locate	potife	zuride
_____ /3	Consonant – *le*	stable	grickle	morkle
_____ /3	*r*-controlled	further	tirper	pharbid
_____ /3	Vowel team	outlaw	doipnow	loymaud

6. Spelling

A. Give the student a pencil and a sheet of lined paper. Tell the student: *Listen to each of the words I read and write the **first sound** you hear.* Write the student's responses over the words.

_____/5   fit   map   pen   kid   hand

B. Tell the student: *Listen to each of the words I read and write the **last sound** you hear.* Write the student's responses over the words.

_____/5   rub   fled   leg   sell   less

C. Tell the student: *Listen to each of the words I read and write the **whole word**.*

_____/5   beg   yam   sip   rod   tub

_____/5   train   float   steep   drive   spoon

CORE Phonics Survey
Student Material

1.

D	A	N	S	X	Z	J	L	H
T	Y	E	C	O	M	R	P	W
K	U	G	B	F	Q	V	I	

2.

d	a	n	s	x	z	j	l	h
t	y	e	c	o	m	r	p	w
k	u	g	b	f	q	v	i	

3.

d	l	n	s	x	z	j
t	y	p	c	h	m	r
k	w	g	b	f	q	v

4.

e	i	a	o	u

5. Reading and Decoding

A.

| sit | cat | get | but | hot |
| vot | fut | dit | ket | lat |

B.

| when | chop | thin | shut | match |
| wheck | shom | thax | phitch | chud |

C.

stop	trap	quick	spell	plan
stig	brab	qued	snop	dran
ring	fast	sank	limp	held
mang	nast	wunk	kimp	jelt

D.

| tape | Pete | cute | paid | feet |
| pofe | bine | joad | vay | soat |

3

E.

few	down	toy	hawk	coin
moit	rew	fout	zoy	bawk

F.

bark	horn	chirp	roar	cold
ferm	murd	gair	dall	chail

G.

kidnap	pugnad	quibrap
compete	slifnate	prubkine
depend	sunop	wopam
zero	zubo	yodu
locate	potife	zuride
stable	grickle	morkle
further	tirper	pharbid
outlaw	doipnow	loymaud

Percentage Scores Chart

Number Correct	Total Number of Items					
	5	10	20	25	30	40
1	20%	10%	5%	4%	3%	3%
2	40%	20%	10%	8%	7%	5%
3	60%	30%	15%	12%	10%	8%
4	80%	40%	20%	16%	13%	10%
5	100%	50%	25%	20%	17%	13%
6		60%	30%	24%	20%	15%
7		70%	35%	28%	23%	18%
8		80%	40%	32%	27%	20%
9		90%	45%	36%	30%	23%
10		100%	50%	40%	33%	25%
11			55%	44%	37%	28%
12			60%	48%	40%	30%
13			65%	52%	43%	33%
14			70%	56%	47%	35%
15			75%	60%	50%	38%
16			80%	64%	53%	40%
17			85%	68%	57%	43%
18			90%	72%	60%	45%
19			95%	76%	63%	48%
20			100%	80%	67%	50%
21				84%	70%	53%
22				88%	73%	55%
23				92%	77%	58%
24				96%	80%	60%
25				100%	83%	63%
26					87%	65%
27					90%	68%
28					93%	70%
29					97%	73%
30					100%	75%
31						78%
32						80%
33						83%
34						85%
35						88%
36						90%
37						93%
38						95%
39						98%
40						100%

Reading Placement Tests / Grade 1